You Are Not Alone

Khyla "Kye" Rush

Published by Power in the Bloodline Publishing, 2026.

YOU ARE NOT ALONE

First edition. January 15, 2026.

ISBN: 979-8994212905

Written by Khyla "Kye" Rush.

Table of Contents

DEDICATION

———

For my beautiful twin daughters,

Aeja AnnReese Rush and Alaeja Keeyoni Rush,

born into heaven on February 20, 2013.

Your brief presence changed me forever.

This book is my love letter to you

and to every parent who has known the ache of empty arms.

To my daughter who came after,

a light that reminded me joy can bloom again.

And to my son, my miracle gift,

proof that life can surprise us with love even after deep loss.

May these words remind us all:

even in grief, we are never truly alone.

ACKNOWLEDGMENTS

To my daughter, whose laughter reminded me that joy could still live in my heart.

To my son, a miracle I once believed could never be. You are both living testaments of love and hope after loss.

To my family and friends who stood by me in the silence, when words could not heal, but presence did. Thank you.

A special acknowledgment to Joseph A. Desautels, MD, OB/GYN, Montgomery, AL 36117, for your care, compassion, and steady hands during the most fragile chapter of my life.

And to every parent who has carried the weight of grief in their chest, this book is for you, with you, and beside you.

With love,

Khyla Rush

CHAPTER 1

―――

THE DAY EVERYTHING CHANGED

I did not wake up that morning thinking my world would split in two.

I got dressed, I moved through the day, and the sun still rose as if it did not know what was coming.

No one prepares you for how quickly life can go from full of promise to hollow in a single breath. One moment, there was a future I had already begun to love. The next, there was only stillness where movement used to be.

I remember the coldness of the room, the way my hands would not stop shaking. I remember how the words felt like they were falling from far away. I am sorry, there is no heartbeat. They did not land in my ears at first. They floated around me, heavy and waiting for me to believe them.

It was not just the loss of a baby. It was the loss of the version of me who thought love and hope were enough to keep something alive. It was the loss of the laughter I had already imagined, the first words, the warm weight in my arms.

And in that moment, I learned that grief is not loud. It does not come screaming. It seeps in like water through cracks until you are soaked through and do not remember what it felt like to be dry.

I wish I could say I cried right away. I did not. I sat in silence, staring at the wall, as if staring long enough could make the truth change its mind. The tears came later in waves I could not control, at times I did not expect. That day became a before and after in my life.

Before, I carried a heartbeat inside me.

After, I carried only the memory of it.

And yet, even in that first shattering moment, somewhere deep inside me, so deep I could not feel it yet, a small truth was forming. This love, though it would ache, would not die with my children.

CHAPTER 2

———

THE SILENCE AFTERWARDS

After the doctors left and the room was empty, there was a silence so thick I could almost touch it.

It was not the kind of silence that brings peace.

It was the kind that presses down on your chest and makes the air feel too heavy to breathe.

I could hear everything. The hum of the machines, the faint squeak of shoes in the hallway, the ticking of a clock I wished would stop. Every sound seemed to remind me that the world was still moving even though mine had stopped.

When I left the hospital, the world outside was loud again. Cars, voices, life everywhere. But inside me, it was quiet. Too quiet. My body still felt pregnant in ways my heart could not bear to acknowledge. And that emptiness did not just live in my womb. It echoed through my thoughts and my future.

Home was not the same.

The clothes I had bought, folded neatly and waiting, seemed to stare at me. I avoided certain rooms, certain drawers, certain moments. I did not have the strength to look hope in the face.

People did not know what to say, so most said nothing at all. Their silence felt like distance even when they meant well. Others filled the space with words that were supposed to comfort but felt like salt on an open wound.

It is God's plan.

You can try again.

At least you know you can get pregnant.

I knew they were trying.

I also knew they did not understand.

In the quiet moments, the ache was loud. Late at night. Early in the morning. In the shower. The silence had its own language. It told me what I had lost again and again.

I used to think silence meant nothing was happening. I was wrong.

In those heavy days, my heart was slowly learning the shape of my grief.

And even though I could not see it yet, somewhere in that silence, a seed of healing had already been planted.

CHAPTER 3

———

GRIEF'S MANY FACES

Grief does not wear just one face.

It shifts.

It changes.

Sometimes within minutes.

Sometimes without warning.

One day you might feel heavy with sadness. The next, you might feel nothing at all. Both are real. Both are valid.

Some mornings I woke up with a lump in my throat before my feet touched the floor. The tears waited like an old friend I did not want to see. Other days, I moved through the hours almost normally until a sound, a smell, or a stranger smiling at their baby cracked me open.

I learned that grief is not just crying.

It is the numbness that makes you stare at the wall for an hour without noticing.

It is the anger that rises at nothing and everything.

At life.

At your own body.

At how unfair it all is.

It is the guilt that whispers, What did I do wrong, even when you know you did everything you could.

It is the envy that hits when someone announces a pregnancy, followed by the shame for feeling that way.

No one tells you how exhausting grief is. It takes energy to hold sadness. It takes energy to keep breathing when the air feels thick. Some days, I had nothing left to give.

But hear me clearly.

Every emotion is part of the process.

Grief is messy. It is not linear. There is no correct way to feel.

Some days you may find yourself laughing and then feel guilty for forgetting your pain. But joy does not mean you stopped loving your baby. Joy means you are still alive. It means the part of you that knows how to love life is still inside you.

Grief will continue changing shape. Sometimes soft. Sometimes roaring. But every version is proof of your love.

And love never disappears.

CHAPTER 4

———

PERMISSION TO FEEL

If I could sit with you right now, I would take your hands in mine, look you in the eyes, and tell you this.

You are allowed to feel everything.

You do not have to be strong all the time.

You do not have to hold it together so others feel comfortable around you.

You do not have to rush your healing because someone thinks you have grieved long enough.

You are allowed to cry until your body shakes.

You are allowed to feel angry at the situation, at your own body, at the unfairness of it all.

You are allowed to feel numb, like the world is moving around you while you are standing still.

And you are also allowed to laugh.

To enjoy a sunny day.

To dream about the future without guilt.

Grief and joy can live in the same heart, even on the same day.

No one else gets to decide what your grief should look like.

This is your love.

This is your loss.

This is your healing.

If today feels heavy, let it be heavy.

If tomorrow feels light, let it be light.

There is no timeline.

There is no getting over it.

There is only learning to carry it in a way that does not crush you.

I used to believe that letting go of the pain meant letting go of the baby.

But I have learned that healing does not mean forgetting.

It means making room for other parts of yourself to live again.

Your love will never leave.

Your memories will never fade.

And your permission to feel everything will be the bridge that carries you through the hardest days.

So if no one has told you lately:

Take the nap.

Cancel the plans.

Cry in the grocery store if you need to.

Hold the blanket close.

Write their name in the sand.

Talk to them out loud.

Do whatever your heart needs.

You do not have to apologize for the way you grieve.

YOU ARE NOT ALONE

You are not too much.

You are human.

And that is enough.

CHAPTER 5

———

THE UNSEEN COMPANIONS

Even though our arms are empty, our hearts are still full.

The love we carry for our babies does not disappear when they are no longer here in the way we hoped.

It shifts.

It changes.

It becomes something we hold in ways the world cannot see, but we can feel every single day.

For a long time, I thought moving forward meant leaving my baby behind.

But I have learned that they walk with me still.

Not in body, but in spirit.

Not in sound, but in memory.

Not in sight, but in love.

They are the quiet presence in moments no one else notices.

The soft reminder inside your chest.

The warmth that rises when you need comfort most.

You might feel them when you hear a certain song.

When you see a certain flower.

When sunlight finds you on a hard day.

YOU ARE NOT ALONE

You might talk to them when you are alone, and even if the words are spoken only in your heart, I believe they hear you.

There are gentle ways to honor that connection and make it real in your everyday life.

• Write them letters on days that feel heavy or full of love.

• Create a memory box with ultrasound photos or small items that hold meaning.

• Light a candle on special days and let the flame represent the light they brought into your life.

• Plant something in their honor and watch it grow as a living symbol of continued love.

• Wear a charm or piece of jewelry that helps you feel close to them.

These acts are not about holding on to pain.

They are about holding on to love.

Some people may not understand.

They might think you are dwelling on the past.

But remembering is part of healing.

It is not living in what was.

It is weaving their presence into what is.

Your baby existed.

Your baby mattered.

And every time you honor them, you remind the world and yourself that love cannot be measured by time.

No matter how short their life may have been, your child left a mark.

And you carry that mark with grace, even in the moments when you feel anything but strong.

They are still yours.

You are still theirs.

Love keeps you connected.

Always.

CHAPTER 6

―――――

LEANING INTO SUPPORT

Grief can make you feel like you are on an island.

You can be surrounded by people, yet still feel completely alone.

There is fear in letting others close during the most vulnerable moments.

You may worry they will not understand.

You may worry they will say the wrong thing.

You may want to protect your heart from any more pain.

But you were not meant to carry this alone.

Some people will show up quietly and consistently.

They may not have perfect words, but they will offer presence.

They may not know what to say, but they will stay anyway.

Support can look like:

• A friend sitting beside you in silence

• A warm meal placed at your door

• Someone offering to drive you to an appointment

• A text message that simply says, I am here

• Someone who listens without trying to fix your grief

You are allowed to lean on people who make you feel safe.

You are allowed to choose who gets close to your heart.

Not everyone earns access to your healing space, and that is okay.

You can tell people what you need.

You can say, Please listen without trying to solve anything.

You can say, I need some space today.

You can say, I need help, and I do not know how to ask for it.

Support does not erase grief.

But it can soften the weight long enough for you to breathe again.

There will be days when you feel strong on your own.

There will be days when you need someone to hold you together.

Both kinds of days are worthy.

Both kinds of days are normal.

Let the ones who love you help carry the heaviness when it becomes too much.

Healing is not about independence.

Healing is about connection, care, and allowing people in where the pain lives.

You deserve to be held.

You deserve to be supported.

You deserve to feel less alone.

Your heart is still learning how to exist in this new world.

Let someone offer a hand when the ground feels unsteady.

CHAPTER 7

―――

WHEN THE WEIGHT SHIFTS

There is no announcement when healing begins.

No bright sign that says, You made it.

No sudden moment where everything feels normal again.

Healing comes quietly.

It comes in the mornings when you realize you can breathe without crying first.

It comes in the laughter you did not expect.

It comes in the moments when grief loosens its grip just enough for you to feel a spark of light.

For me, the shift was small at first.

A day when the ache did not throb the entire time.

A night when I could fall asleep without tears on my pillow.

I did not trust it at first.

I wondered if the softening meant I was forgetting.

I wondered if it meant my love was fading.

But healing does not mean letting go of your baby.

Healing means letting go of the belief that pain is the only way to honor them.

The weight slowly changes.

You still carry the love.

You still remember every detail.

The difference is the grief no longer controls every breath.

What shifting can look like:

• Smiling without guilt

• Being able to talk about your baby without breaking apart

• Noticing beauty again

• Feeling hope return in small pieces

• Wanting to create, dream, or explore again

Some days the weight will feel light.

Other days it will feel heavier again.

This is not failure.

This is healing.

There is no going back to who you were before.

Loss reshapes you.

But there is a version of you ahead with more strength, more compassion, and more depth than you ever imagined.

The love remains.

The bond remains.

The weight just becomes easier to carry.

Let yourself notice the shift.

Let yourself welcome the softness.

Your baby would want your heart to feel light again,

even if only one moment at a time.

CHAPTER 8

———

LOVE BEYOND TIME

Before loss, I believed love needed time to grow.

I thought you needed years of memories and moments to hold onto.

But I learned that love can be eternal,

even when time is short.

I loved my babies the moment I knew they existed.

That love has never stopped growing,

not for a single heartbeat.

Love does not fade because a life was brief.

Love does not shrink because memories are few.

Love is not bound by days or hours.

Your child is a part of you forever.

Their presence continues

in every breath you take,

in every tear that falls,

in every corner of your heart that aches and heals.

Love begins before birth.

Love continues after death.

Love has no ending.

YOU ARE NOT ALONE

How love lives on:

- Through the way your heart has expanded

- Through the compassion you now carry for others

- Through the strength you did not know you had

- Through the dreams you continue to chase

- Through every time you speak their name

There will always be a part of your heart that aches,

but there will also be a part that glows.

Your baby has given you a love so big

it could never disappear.

They changed you.

They shaped you.

They still guide you.

There is no timeline on love.

There is no limit on connection.

There is no ending to the bond between a parent and child.

And even when the world cannot see them,

you feel them.

That is love.

That is forever.

CHAPTER 9

———

L IVING WITH LIGHT AGAIN
Healing does not come with a countdown.

It comes in moments.

Slow and gentle.

Quiet and unexpected.

For a long time, the world felt dim to me.

Like joy was something that belonged to everyone else.

Like smiling meant I was forgetting.

Like laughter was disrespectful to my grief.

But grief taught me something powerful.

Light and sorrow can exist together.

Your heart is big enough to hold both.

There will come a day

when you notice the sun shining a little brighter,

or you catch yourself laughing without trying,

or you realize your shoulders are not as heavy.

You may feel guilty when this happens.

You may question whether you are allowed

to feel warmth again.

YOU ARE NOT ALONE

You are.

Light returning is not betrayal.

It is love surviving.

It is proof their life changed you

in a way that continues to grow.

Ways to welcome light again:

• Enjoy something simple that once made you smile

• Talk about your baby in moments of joy

• Celebrate the love instead of the loss

• Say yes to new memories

• Allow yourself to breathe without pain

Your healing does not erase your child.

Your joy does not replace your love.

Your future does not abandon your past.

It all exists together.

And that is a beautiful kind of strength.

Grief will always be part of your story,

but so will love,

so will hope,

so will life.

You deserve days that feel warm again.

You deserve laughter,

peace,

soft mornings,

and dreams that still come true.

Even as you carry their memory,

you are allowed to live fully,

because they lived,

and because you still do.

CHAPTER 10

———

L ETTERS TO THE READERS

These letters are for the moments when your heart speaks louder than words.

Return to them whenever you need a hand to hold.

Letter One

On the Days You Can't Get Out of Bed

Sweetheart,

today your only job is to breathe.

You don't have to rise like a warrior.

You don't have to move mountains.

You are alive.

You are trying.

And that is more than enough.

Letter Two

When Guilt Tries to Take Over

You did everything you could.

You loved with your whole body and soul.

Guilt is a liar, one that grief often sends.

Let it pass through, not root inside you.

Your love has always been pure.

Letter Three

When You Feel Numb

Numbness is not the absence of love.

It is your heart taking a break

from breaking.

This is how your mind protects you

until you can feel again.

Rest inside the quiet.

Letter Four

When Joy Surprises You

If you laugh, smile, or feel light,

that doesn't mean you are forgetting.

That is love remembering itself.

Let joy stay when it finds you.

Your baby would want that for you.

Letter Five

On the Loneliest Nights

Close your eyes.

Imagine their tiny hand wrapped in yours.

Feel their presence in the stillness.

Love does not leave.

Even here, even now,

they are closer than breath.

Letter Six

When Tears Come Without Warning

Let them fall.

Each tear is a piece of love

making room inside your heart

for light to enter again.

Crying is not a setback.

It is release.

Letter Seven

When the World Moves On Without You

Take your time.

Your timeline is sacred.

Grief does not follow calendars.

You are not behind.

You are healing in your own way.

Letter Eight

When You Doubt Your Strength

Look at you.

Still standing.

Still loving.

Still breathing through the ache.

That is strength.

Even in your softest moments.

Letter Nine

When You Miss Them Most

Say their name.

Hold their story.

Remember their impact.

That love, that ache,

everything that hurts

is everything that mattered.

Letter Ten

When You're Ready for Hope

Hope doesn't replace grief.

It sits beside it.

Hand in hand.

Heart in heart.

You are allowed to keep both.

CHAPTER 11

———

HEALING PRACTICES

Healing is not about forgetting.

It is not about being strong every day.

Healing is learning to live with love and grief together in the same heart.

Here are gentle practices you can return to whenever the weight feels too heavy.

1. Hand Over Heart Breathing

Place your hand over your heart.

Close your eyes if it feels safe.

Inhale slowly for four seconds.

Hold for two.

Exhale for six.

Let the breath soften the ache instead of pushing it away.

Repeat until your chest loosens, even just a little.

2. Journal Prompts for Release

Write without judgment.

Write without worrying if the words make sense.

Your heart knows what it needs to say.

Try:

• Today my grief feels like

- If I could say anything to my baby right now

- One memory I want to carry forever

- Something I am proud of myself for today

- My baby taught me

Let the page hold what you have been carrying alone.

3. A Memory That Grows

Plant something in their honor.

A flower.

A tree.

Even a small plant by the window.

As it grows, let it remind you that love continues even in places that have known loss.

4. A Candle for the Heavy Days

Light a candle when the silence gets loud.

Watch the flame flicker.

Imagine it whispering.

You are still here.

And so is the love.

5. A Safe Place Visualization

Find a quiet space.

Breathe gently.

Picture a place where you feel safe.

YOU ARE NOT ALONE

Warm.

Protected.

Imagine your baby there too in whatever form brings peace.

A ray of light.

A tiny hand in yours.

A butterfly resting near your heart.

Stay as long as you need.

You can visit this place whenever the storm rises again.

6. Gentle Affirmations for Grieving Hearts

Read these aloud even if your voice trembles.

- My love is stronger than my pain

- Healing does not mean forgetting

- I am allowed to rest

- My grief is real and valid

- I am still whole

- I am learning to live again

Grief is not a straight line.

Some days you will feel light.

Some days you will crawl.

Some days you will only breathe.

Every version of you is doing the best it can.

And that is enough.

CLOSING

YOU ARE NOT ALONE

Thank you for holding these pages with me.

Thank you for breathing through each word, even the ones that hurt to read.

It takes courage to look grief in the eyes and say,

I am still here.

There will always be moments when the ache returns like a tide, but that does not mean you are going backward. It means the love is still alive.

Your baby is still yours.

Your heart is still capable of light.

Your story is still unfolding.

On the days that feel heavy, remember this.

You have survived every hard moment so far.

You have learned how to carry what once crushed you.

You have made it here, to this moment, with your love still intact.

That is strength.

That is motherhood.

That is grace.

If you ever forget, let these final words remind you.

You are seen.

You are held.

You are loved.

YOU ARE NOT ALONE

You are not alone.

A Note to the Reader

Take your time as you continue your own healing.

There is no finish line to reach.

There is no right way to grieve.

You carry a love that changed you forever, and that love will continue to grow into the life you are still meant to live.

Your baby's story did not end on the day their tiny heartbeat faded.

It lives in you.

In every breath.

In every step forward.

In every moment of courage and care.

May you always know this.

Their life mattered.

And so does yours.

About the Author

Khyla "Kye" Rush is a mother, writer, and healing advocate whose work is rooted in love, loss, and resilience. After experiencing miscarriage and stillbirth, she found herself searching for words that could hold grief without rushing it and comfort without minimizing pain.

You Are Not Alone was written from lived experience, for parents navigating the quiet, heavy spaces of loss. Through gentle reflection and honest emotion, Khyla hopes to offer connection, validation, and a reminder that grief does not have to be carried alone.

Her work centers on healing, remembrance, and honoring the enduring bond between parent and child.

POWER
IN THE
BLOODLINE
PUBLISHING
Where pain becomes purpose

About the Publisher

Power in the Bloodline Publishing is an independent publishing imprint dedicated to stories of healing, resilience, and generational restoration. Its mission is to amplify voices that speak truth, nurture hope, and remind readers of the strength that lives within their stories.

www.ingramcontent.com/pod-product-compliance
Lightning Source LLC
Chambersburg PA
CBHW031009090426
42737CB00008B/742